traditional KOBUJUTSU

Professor Robert Clark · 9th Dan

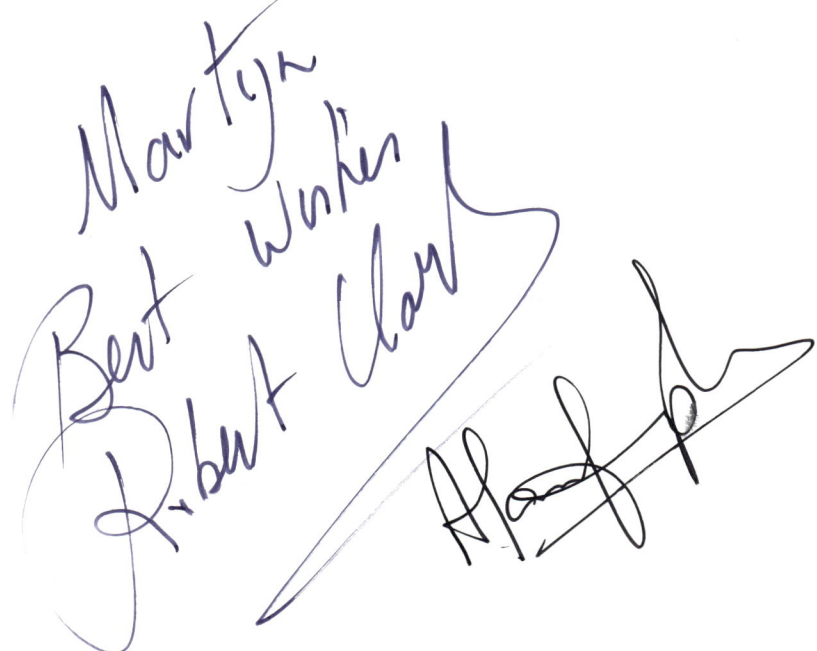

A & C Black · London

First published 1996 by
A & C Black (Publishers) Ltd
35 Bedford Row, London WC1R 4JH

Copyright © 1996 by Robert Clark

ISBN 0 7136 4381 1

All rights reserved. No part of this publication
may be reproduced in any form or by any
means – graphic, electronic or mechanical,
including photocopying, recording, taping or
information storage and retrieval systems -
without the prior permission in writing of the
publishers.

A CIP catalogue record for this book
is available from the British Library.

Distributed in the USA by
The Talman Company
131 Spring Street
New York, NY 10012

Designed and typeset by
Alan Hamp @ Design for Books

Printed and bound in Great Britain by
Hillman Printers (Frome) Ltd, Frome, Somerset

Contents

Introduction 5
  Kobujutsu 5
  History 5
  The tonfa 5
  The rice flail 6
  Mastering martial weapons 6
  Training kobujutsu within the
    World Kobujutsu Organisation 7

Etiquette and WKO rules 8
  Etiquette 8
  The WKO rules 9
  Traditional weapons and
    the law 10

Training safely 11

Choosing your kobujutsu club 12

Clothing 13

Grading 14

Warming up/cooling down 15

The tonfa 17
  Introduction 17
  The tonfa kata 17

The nunchaku 50
  Introduction 50
  The nunchaku kata 50

The police tonfa 75
  Introduction 75
  Applications 75

The nunchaku – advanced
  applications 86

And finally … 96

Acknowledgements

Both the author and the publishers would like to thank Alan Campbell, Robert Clark's willing partner, and David Mitchell for his assistance in the production of this book.
All photography by Martin Sellars.

Robert Clark has also written the complete syllabus of the World Jiu Jitsu Federation. It is published in three volumes by A & C Black.

For a full list of A & C Black's martial arts publications, please write to: Martial Arts Books, A & C Black, 35 Bedford Row, London WC1R 4JH.

Introduction

Kobujutsu

Kobujutsu is a Japanese term meaning 'old martial arts', though today the general usage of the term has narrowed to cover unusual Oriental weapons. You may encounter the word *kobudo*, which means 'old martial way'. The two practices are almost indistinguishable from each other, the main difference being that kobujutsu teaches you how to use weapons effectively whereas kobudo teaches you how to be a more self-disciplined person through practising with weapons. The methods are essentially the same; only the objectives are different.

History

Until the early seventeenth century, when the island of Okinawa was annexed by the Japanese from the nearby mainland, it possessed its own military traditions based on a blending of indigenous, Chinese and Japanese systems. Unarmed and covertly-armed fighting systems were unusually prevalent since in 1470 an Okinawan royal edict forbade weapons to all except the king's officers. Without an effective police force to protect them, the peasants were obliged to use agricultural and domestic tools as weapons.

Skills in using these tools as weapons developed into traditions, traditions which exist to the present day. An essential part of these traditions is the training sequences, or *kata*, which were devised to familiarise users with the weapons' characteristics. While many tools were used in this way, this book concerns itself with just two: the rice grinder handles, or *tonfa*, and the rice flail, or *nunchaku*.

The tonfa

Rice grinder handles (*tonfa*) are old domestic implements which, with a little training, can become formidable weapons. They consist of a pair of flattened, heavy wood batons with a peg projecting at right angles near to one end. Typically they were held by the pegs, with the longer part of the baton laying against the forearm and the butt end projecting forward. The butt gave extension and force to a punch while the baton protected the forearm from impact injury. Held this way, the tonfa could be swung out in a circle, swivelling on the peg so the baton flipped forward to strike the side of the opponent's head.

That the tonfa is a very versatile weapon is attested to by the fact that they are now used by many police forces in place of plain batons. Police tonfas are typically longer than the traditional type and they are used singly, except in Russia.

Ideally, tonfa batons should be made to measure so the peg is of the right length to be grasped firmly. The longer baton should extend as far along the forearm as the elbow; any shorter and it will not be able to fully protect the arm from powerful swinging attacks.

The rice flail

Perhaps the most famous of all the Okinawan covert weapons is the rice flail, or *nunchaku*. The original rice flail was a long-handled slat to which a shorter slat was attached by a fabric hinge. This allowed two-dimensional movement only and an unadapted flail is of little use as a weapon. The developed flail has batons of equal weight – they have to be or their unequal ballistics cause problems. Effective batons are made from hardwood and have a round or octagonal cross section. *Safety-chuks* are made from lightweight plastic tube, covered in a dense foam. Use these to practise catches and swap-over sequences because they cause no injury when they hit you. As you become more skilful, make your own nunchakus from soft wood and this will give you a useful intermediate between the safety-chuk and the real thing.

The flexible link between the two batons has a critical length which you decide after trying various lengths of cord. You can use chain to link the batons though this is heavier and makes the ballistics more complex. There are problems, too, with the universal joint and much used chain rice flails sometimes come apart. I recommend using nylon braided cord threaded through well smoothed and relieved holes. Sharp-edged holes cause rapid fraying of the cord, so open them out!

Rice flail training katas teach how to control the swinging baton, transferring it smoothly from hand to hand as it weaves a wall of whirling wood around the user, through which nothing can pass.

Mastering martial weapons

The road to excellence in kobujutsu practice is a long and hard one which makes great demands on both the body and the mind of the student. Physical fitness comes through practice but mental fitness is sometimes harder to develop.

First of all, kobujutsu practice calls for patience and persistence – to keep working at techniques until they are right. Secondly, kobujutsu demands a true humility which comes about only through self-knowledge. By all means be moderately pleased with yourself for reaching the standard you hold, but never be envious or contemptuous about the standard of others. Thirdly, kobujutsu requires students to have an enquiring mind that looks closely at what is being taught. Don't be content merely to copy – understand as well – because knowledge allows you to develop your practice.

Training kobujutsu within the World Kobujutsu Organisation

Founded in 1993, the World Kobujutsu Organisation (WKO) represents the culmination of 30 years of general martial art experience. That is, three decades of study, development and refinement in both martial techniques, and in the methods of teaching them. The WKO's Chief International Technical Director is Robert Clark, the author of this book.

The WKO is totally committed to the art of kobujutsu, to its continuing technical development and to teaching the art to anyone who is willing to learn. There are no exceptions to these commitments. From children and teenagers to elderly people and the physically disadvantaged, the WKO opens its doors to all. Whether you are looking to improve your martial skills or trying to increase your fitness, agility, awareness and self-confidence, the WKO can meet your needs.

Kobujutsu practice underlies many of the martial disciplines practised today, making it a valuable add-on to your current practice. Through practising it, you may well discover the purpose behind many of those moves in your patterns which have puzzled you for years.

The WKO offers the perfect philosophy, the perfect environment and the perfect opportunity to learn, understand and practise kobujutsu. There is only one place to experience the world of kobujutsu and that is through the World Kobujutsu Organisation.

Etiquette and WKO rules

Etiquette

Kobujutsu practice begins and ends with courtesy. If you do not respect your teacher, then how can you have respect for yourself for learning under him/her? If you do not respect your fellow students, how can you expect them to train safely and effectively with you?

Insistence by the WKO on just one type of kobujutsu uniform and badge ensures that no social distinctions creep into the training hall. Everyone looks the same and everyone is treated the same – with courtesy. Not only is this courtesy expressed in the form of polite attention to what the coach is saying, it is also expressed by means of the bow.

When no-one is in the training hall as you enter, pause at the entrance and face the centre of the room. Put your heels together and your hands flat against the front of your thighs. This posture is known as 'attention stance'. Then perform a standing bow. If other people are in the training hall, then bow towards the senior grade.

Don't bow too far, just incline your upper body forward. Make the bow smooth and hesitate at the lowest point for a count of two before straightening up again. As befits the follower of any true fighting art, you should always be on the lookout for attack, so never look down at the floor as you bow. Once you make the bow, you can step into the training hall. Bow also when leaving the hall, even if only for a short interval.

The class is called together by a senior person and arranges itself into lines according to grade. Training tunics are adjusted until they are tidy and the following ritual takes place when activity has died down.

- Begin by standing in attention stance.
- Keep your back straight as you lower your left knee to the mat.
- Lower your right knee and sit back on your calves.

Your ankles are now fully extended, so the feet are pointed. Ankle flexibility is the limiting factor in this position and you may need to do some homework, perhaps by kneeling on cushions over gradually longer periods until you can hold the position. Then, when you are settled into kneeling position ...

- Slide your hands forward and palm-downwards on to the mat. Bend your elbows and lean forward in a smooth movement, but keep your eyes on the coach – don't look down at the mat!
- Pause at the lowest point, then return smoothly to a straight-back position.
- Return to a standing position by first raising the left knee, then the right. Stand with your feet together once more and perform a standing bow to the coach.

If you miss the opening ritual described above, then pause at the door of the training hall and wait for the coach to call you on to the mat. Go through your warm-up exercises quietly in a corner of the room and then perform the kneeling bow. Remain in kneeling position and await the coach's invitation to join the lesson.

Pay close attention when the coach is speaking and don't lounge against walls or sprawl yourself over the mat. When the coach is showing the class a technique, make sure you can see the demonstration clearly. Ask questions when the coach invites you to, otherwise do not interrupt what is being demonstrated. If you are chosen to assist the coach, don't make fatuous remarks or move about without permission. If for any reason you are told to sit down at the side of the mat, then tuck your feet under you so people don't trip over them. Don't discuss techniques loudly with your partner and only practise what you have been shown.

WKO clubs train on a matted surface and under no circumstances should you or your guest(s) walk on the mat with shoes on! Walk around the edge of the mat, or leave your shoes at the entrance to the training hall. Do not smoke, eat, or talk noisily.

Kobujutsu practice involves working in close proximity with another person so personal hygiene is very important. Tie long hair back with an elastic band because hair grips and metal clasps are dangerous. Ear-rings, necklaces and jewellery of all kinds must be removed and stored safely for the duration of the lesson. Spectacles should not be worn, though you can wear soft contact lenses, which are your own responsibility. Keep your finger- and toe-nails short.

The WKO rules

Read and memorise the following regulations because they are standard in WKO training halls all over the world.

(1) The coach is concerned with your safety and with the correct performance of technique. Obey his/her directions at all times.
(2) Students may enter and leave the training hall only with the coach's permission.
(3) Instruction may only take place under the direct supervision of a properly qualified WKO coach. Only currently enrolled members may receive tuition.
(4) Gradings may only take place under the direction of the National Coach of the WKO or his delegated nominees.
(5) Members of the WKO must not misuse their knowledge of kobujutsu.
(6) Kobujutsu techniques must not be demonstrated outside of a training hall.

(7) Members of the WKO may not participate in any display of kobujutsu without prior permission from the WKO.

(8) Smoking is not allowed in any WKO training hall.

(9) Outdoor shoes must not be worn in the training hall.

(10) All injuries, whether pre-existing or incurred during a session, must be reported to the club coach.

(11) The WKO reserves the right to terminate the membership of any person that the WKO considers unsuitable for martial art training.

(12) Violation of any of these rules renders a member liable to disciplinary procedures, which may include expulsion of that member from the WKO.

Traditional weapons and the law

Martial art films have done much to focus attention on traditional weapons and today people tend to have a distorted view of their effectiveness. If you openly carry a traditional weapon in a public place, then you are liable to be arrested and charged. As the law now stands, you must be able to show good reason for carrying something like a rice flail. This being the case, you should always wrap your weapon in your training tunic and then put the tunic into a closed bag.

Carry your WKO licence with you and go directly from home to the club, and directly back again. Don't be tempted to go to a football match carrying the weapon in your training bag! Be prepared to produce your WKO licence for inspection by a police officer; this, along with the careful way in which you have concealed the weapon, may serve to convince the officer that you have a good reason for having it in your possession. However, your WKO licence will have little value if you are found twirling the weapon about in a public place.

Training safely

Kobujutsu can be quite a strenuous activity, especially for someone coming into it cold from a sedentary job. So check whether you're fit enough to practise. This is particularly important for novices over the age of 40.

Let the coach know about any health conditions at the time of your application for membership of the WKO, or as soon as the conditions are diagnosed, whichever is the sooner. Telling the coach about your health condition allows him to check your performance and he may spot the onset of symptoms before you do.

The term 'health conditions' means, for example, epilepsy, migraines, asthma, heart problems, or blood-clotting disorders. Haemophilia is the only health condition that positively disbars you (for your own safety!) from practising the kobujutsu described in this syllabus. Consult your doctor if you are unsure whether or not you have a health condition which ought to be disclosed to the coach.

Don't train soon after eating a large meal. This is because the process of digestion uses up a lot of blood which is otherwise required by the exercising muscles – including the heart – and cramp may result.

Certain types of virus infections can have serious side effects on heart muscle, so avoid sharp bangs on the chest and sudden training spurts if you have a cold.

Don't train too close to unshielded windows, glass doors, benches, pillars, or the edge of the mat. Take extra care if you are larger than your partner because big people generate a lot of power without being aware of it. Finally, don't leave training bags or unused kit where it can be tripped over.

Choosing your kobujutsu club

Choosing the correct kobujutsu club is the most important step you will take in your training career. Pick the wrong one and you could waste many years of hard practice, because not all kobujutsu clubs are good clubs! Unfortunately there is no legal requirement for kobujutsu instructors to be recognised by a competent national body and only a few black belts are properly trained coaches.

If you are not already a member of the WKO, then discover the location of your nearest club by using the contact address given below. If you are already practising in a kobujutsu club, then check it is a member of the WKO by asking the coach whether he/she is registered with the Organisation.

All member clubs of the WKO register their individual students on an annual basis and this means you will receive a WKO licence. The licence is a receipt for the money you paid for registration: if it does not mention the WKO, you have not joined a member club!

The WKO licence contains a valuable insurance policy that not only protects you from the legal consequences of injuring another student, it also covers you against injury and compensates you for the period you are injured. It is therefore essential that you maintain an up-to-date registration by giving in your application form to the club coach **before** your present registration expires.

The address for confirming the location of your nearest WKO club is:

>The World Kobujutsu Organisation
>Barlows Lane
>Fazakerley
>Liverpool
>L9 9EH

When you join a WKO kobujutsu club, you will pay an annual fee which registers you as a member. This annual fee includes a valuable personal accident and third party indemnity insurance, and you should ask the coach for full details about what it covers.

Each time you train you may be required to pay a mat fee. This varies from club to club and it pays for such things as the cost of hiring the premises in which the club trains, etc. The average length of a session is 90 minutes, and it is best to train at least twice a week.

Each time you take a grading you will be required to pay a grading fee. This varies with the grade you are taking. Successful candidates will receive a merit certificate for each grade attained.

Clothing

There is no need to buy a training uniform straight away – a T-shirt and a pair of track-suit bottoms will be fine. At some stage, however, you will want to buy a proper WKO training tunic.

The highly distinctive WKO uniform is of known quality and appearance. If looked after it will last you several years of hard practice, but buy one that is a size too large because it will shrink slightly with subsequent washings. Wash the tunic every week, otherwise it will quickly become unpleasant both for you and your partner. Remember, a tidy appearance shows self-respect and the correct attitude to training, whereas a dirty or ripped suit indicates an uncaring attitude.

Each new tunic is supplied with a belt. Check that it is the right colour for your grade. If not, buy a belt from the club coach. Don't be tempted to dye your old belt. The perspiration produced during training always causes the dye to run and ruin your tunic.

There is a right and a wrong way to tie a belt. Start by wrapping the belt twice around your waist and draw the ends to an equal length. Tuck one end up the inside of both coils and bring it over the top. Then bring the second end across and tuck the first under and through, pulling the knot tight.

Track-suits and flip-flop sandals are useful, especially when you are obliged to walk between the changing room and the practice area. Again, WKO track-suits and flip-flops are available through the club coach.

Buy weapons only through your club coach, otherwise you are likely to pay more and end up with less. WKO-approved weapons have been tested over an extended period and are unlikely to come apart during training (and possibly cause injury). Please note that neither the club coach nor the WKO can be held responsible for accidents arriving out of the use of unauthorised weapons.

Grading

Kobujutsu skills are learned through a ladder of progression known as a grading system. The grading system measures your progress and indicates the level of skill you have reached by means of coloured belts, certificates and entries in your record book.

There are four levels of competence within the WKO syllabus, the highest being the black belt. Each level tests your skill in the use of four weapons – the staff, the tonfa, the nunchaku and the sai.

The following belt colour schemes are used by the WKO.

- Red and white belt: novice grade.
- Blue and white belt: intermediate grade.
- Brown and white belt: advanced intermediate grade.
- Black belt: advanced grade.

Grading examinations are conducted by the National Coach, or by his appointed examiners. Coloured belt gradings can take place in your club or at a regional centre, but all dan gradings are held at the WKO Liverpool headquarters.

In order to take your next grading, you must have:

- completed the required number of training sessions
- completed the required number of special courses
- a current WKO registration
- paid the requisite fee.

Warming up/cooling down

Kobujutsu is a healthy activity which, through its regular practice, generates a whole-body fitness characterised by the ability to train for long periods under light loads, to act explosively when circumstances require it, and to move with agility. Kobujutsu makes no great demands in terms of joint flexibility and neither does it require students to work at near maximum effort over long periods of time. Consequently, there is little need for the long warm-up, cool-down and body preparation programmes found in other martial arts.

Kobujutsu practice stresses the notion of 'health'; that is, the whole body and mind working efficiently and in harmony. This being the case, kobujutsu exercises work the body gently and thoroughly, and always well within its limits. Only a small number of exercises are required to prepare the body and mind for practice, and the most suitable for kobujutsu training come from the Far East.

Perform each exercise in a gentle manner, holding it for at least ten seconds at the point of maximum stretch. Avoid all jerky movements and don't cheat! The exercises are not set out in any particular order, so vary them as you please. Concentrate on what you are doing since this mental discipline forms a part of preparing the mind and body for training.

- Lie on your back and bend your knees. Take hold of your ankles and arch your body upward until only the soles of your feet and the top of your head are supporting your body. Note how the muscles of the chest, abdomen and thighs are stretched. Try and hold this arched position for at least ten seconds – longer if you can manage it.

- This next exercise has a similar training effect to the previous one. Lie on your stomach and bend your knees until you can grasp your ankles. Pull on your ankles, so your body arches. Lift your head and try to look upward. Hold the stretched position for at least ten seconds.

- Lower yourself into a press-up position and bring your fingers together. Drop your hips until your thighs brush the floor. Look upward and hold the stretch for at least ten seconds. Some people then lift the hips clear of the mat, taking them as high as possible, so the spine curves in the reverse direction.

- Lie on your back and raise your feet up and over your head. Brace your hips with your hands, wedging your elbows against the mats. Keep your knees straight and try to touch the mat with the tips of your toes. Hold this position for as long as you can manage.

- The fifth and final exercise of this short series combines shoulder and elbow movement in a simple mobility routine. Lift both arms in front of your upper chest. Circle them one way for a while, then pause and reverse the direction of rotation.

Kobujutsu training is exciting and it is common to finish the lesson on an adrenalin high. This is not a good state for travelling home, so the correct thing to do is to cool down by repeating the above sequence of exercises until you feel relaxed and comfortable.

The tonfa

Introduction

The best way to learn how to use the tonfas is through something we call the *kata*. *Kata* is a Japanese word meaning 'form' or 'pattern'. The kata is a series of attacks and defences against imaginary opponents, devised so that you can hit out at them without the risk of causing injury. There are several kata associated with the tonfa but only the first and most elementary is described here. This first kata includes most of the strikes and blocks which you will make with the tonfas, combining these with suitable body movements and evasions. At first you may not be able to see how exactly these techniques work but don't worry. Learn the steps and the movements first and then go on to the second part of this section when parts of the kata are extracted and their purpose explained.

Begin by learning the kata slowly. It isn't a race! Never let your enthusiasm outstrip your skill because it's much better to begin slowly and correctly, and build speed gradually, as your ability to use the tonfas improves. You will need a little space in which to move about freely and there should be no low light fittings or obstructions to snag the tonfas as they are whirled around.

Even though the kata is an excellent way of learning how to use the tonfas, it cannot teach you anything about the way they react when you actually hit a target with them. Yet this is an important part of training, so at the end of this section you will find a series of appropriate training drills.

The tonfa kata

Fig. 1 Begin from an upright stance with the feet shoulder width apart and the tonfas held by the pegs and along the line of the forearms. Keep your head up, look straight ahead and relax your shoulders.

THE TONFA

Fig. 2 *Above* Step back with the right foot and turn your hips anticlockwise to the left. Extend your right arm forward and bring the left over the top of it and at right angles to it. Draw back your right hand to your side and use this action to help power a left upper forearm block.

Fig. 3 *Above, right* Strongly pull back your left block, twist your right hip forward and strike to midsection with the butt end of the right tonfa.

Fig. 4 *Right* Turn your hips strongly in a clockwise direction, draw back your right fist and cross block with the left tonfa. Allow your feet to swivel naturally and hold the left tonfa vertically.

THE TONFA

Fig. 5 Pull back your left hand and swivel your hips back to the front. Bring your right hand forward, allowing the tonfa to swivel down, and strike the side of the opponent's knee.

Fig. 6 Swivel your hips to the right, pull back the right hand, and return the tonfa along your right forearm. Use this action to help power a rising block performed with the left forearm.

THE TONFA

Fig. 7 Keep your shoulders relaxed, and your arms as they are, during a step forward with your right foot. Even as the step is coming to a stop (and not before!), draw back your left fist to your side, using this action to help power an upward elbow strike made with the right tonfa.

Fig. 8 Turn your hips anticlockwise and lean away, so your body and right leg are in one straight line. Bring your right forearm across your face. The left remains at your side.

THE TONFA

Fig. 9 Strike back with a high parrying movement of the right tonfa.

Fig. 10 Turn your hips further anticlockwise and drop down on to your right knee. Your left arm comes over the top of the right, and you pull the right back to your hip, using this action to help power a lower parry with the left tonfa.

THE TONFA

Fig. 11 Pull the left hand back to your hip and strike upward with the right tonfa, allowing it to swivel up and into the imaginary opponent's groin.

Fig. 12 Return the tonfa to your right side and jab the butt end forward into the opponent's bladder.

Fig. 13 Bring the right tonfa back to your mid-section and change your grip to take the long baton, the peg now projecting inward horizontally. Bring your left arm over the top and lean forward to bar the imaginary opponent's shin with the left tonfa. Slide the peg of the right tonfa behind his Achilles tendon.

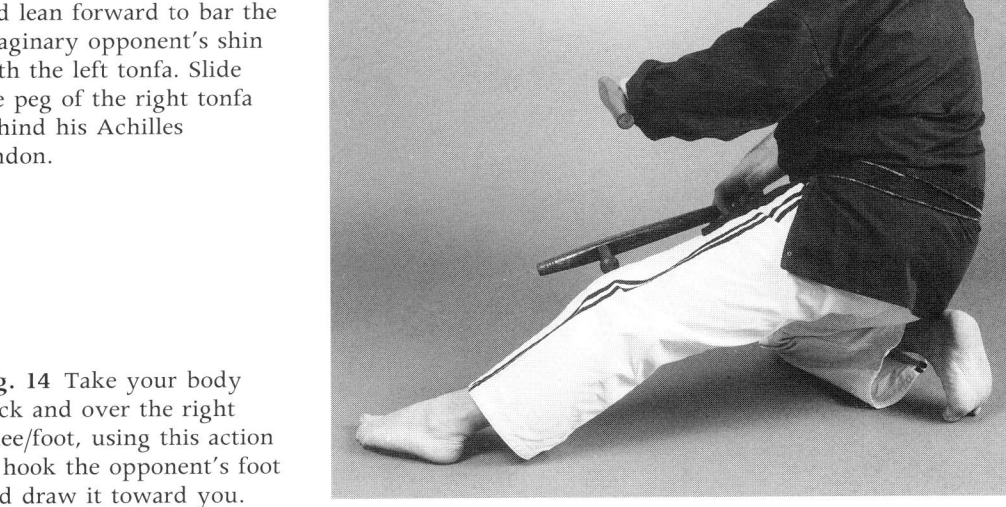

Fig. 14 Take your body back and over the right knee/foot, using this action to hook the opponent's foot and draw it toward you.

THE TONFA

Fig. 15 As the right tonfa comes free, draw it right back in preparation for a downward strike with the peg.

Fig. 16 Complete the strike.

THE TONFA

Fig. 17 *Above* Rise up on your left foot and swivel anticlockwise. The stance is quite narrow and the legs are crossed at this point. Bring the left forearm up in a blocking action and prepare the right tonfa for a strike.

Fig. 18 *Above, right* Hold the left tonfa steady and swing the right tonfa peg into the opponent's ribs.

Fig. 19 *Right* Bring your right forearm back, then step forward with your left leg and bar the opponent across his throat.

THE TONFA

Fig. 20 *Left* Hook the right tonfa peg around the back of the opponent's neck.

Fig. 21 *Below, left* Hold the imaginary opponent firmly as you move your body weight back and slide your left foot across to hook the opponent's leading leg.

Fig. 22 *Below* Lean forward and draw the imaginary opponent down to his knees.

THE TONFA

Fig. 23 Sink down on to your right knee, drawing the opponent toward you by shifting your body weight back over your right knee.

Fig. 24 Release the back of the opponent's neck and draw back the right tonfa ready to perform a downward strike.

Fig. 25 Transfer the body weight forward and draw the left tonfa back to your ribs. Use this action to help power a downward strike with the peg of the right tonfa.

Fig. 26 Raise the right tonfa and turn it until the peg is rotated outward 90°.

THE TONFA

Fig. 27 Drop the tonfa and catch it with your right hand.

Fig. 28 Straighten your left knee and rise, leaning your body away and looking over your right shoulder. The right tonfa is held in a high guard position; the left is against the ribs.

THE TONFA

Fig. 29 Swivel your hips clockwise and perform lower parry with your right forearm.

Fig. 30 Continue turning clockwise. Momentarily bring the left tonfa over the top of the right, then pull it back as you simultaneously perform an upward rising block with your right arm.

THE TONFA

Fig. 31 Then turn your hips anticlockwise and bring your right arm back in preparation for ...

Fig. 32 ... a lower parry.

THE TONFA

Fig. 33 *Above* Draw back your right foot and simultaneously twist clockwise, bringing both forearms back to your sides.

Fig. 34 *Above, right* Step forward with your right foot and thrust both forearms up and to the side of your head in a double block.

Fig. 35 *Right* Retrieve the tonfas, take them back and then bring them together at neck height in a double strike.

THE TONFA

Fig. 36 Draw back your right foot, pulling both batons back to your sides. Then slide forward again with your right foot, bringing both tonfas around for a double horizontal strike to the opponent's temples, with the pegs facing inward.

Fig. 37 Draw back your right foot again and pull both batons to your sides. Slide your right foot back out and then drop down on to your left knee.

THE TONFA

Fig. 38 *Left* Thrust both tonfas out in a double strike, using the butt ends of the batons. The upper tonfa strikes the opponent's throat, the lower tonfa strikes his groin.

Fig. 39 *Below* Lean away to your left and bring the right tonfa across your chest. At the same time, pull back your left fist and strike downward and outward with right lower parry. Lean away to the left.

THE TONFA

Fig. 40 *Above* Draw your right knee in close to the left, and cross the tonfas in front of your chest.

Fig. 41 *Above, right* Drop the tonfas to the front of your knees. Make sure your back is upright and your head held erect. Look straight ahead. Pause in this position for a few seconds, then …

Fig. 42 *Right* … smoothly raise your left knee, resting the tonfa on it.

THE TONFA

Fig. 43 Resume a standing position with your feet shoulder width apart. Move both tonfas in circles so they cross in front of the chest.

Fig. 44 Return to the ready position from which your started.

Applications of the techniques used in the kata
In addition to its use as a baton, the tonfa also reinforces the user's fist and forearm.

Fig. 45 Here the defender has been attacked by an opponent wielding a length of metal pipe. Trying to stop the pipe in this way without the tonfa would almost certainly result in injury to your forearm. You can simply bring the tonfa into the strike, or move it powerfully against the strike in the manner of the so-called 'active armour' of tanks. If the opponent is using a heavy metal bar, then its impact may drive your forearm back. Reduce the chance of this happening by meeting the bar at an angle. The bar then hits the angled tonfa and is re-directed. Having said that, don't re-direct the deflected bar into yourself!

Fig. 46 The advantage of using two tonfas is that having blocked the metal bar, you can then drive the butt of the other into the opponent's mid-section. Used in this way, the tonfa augments your punching action by impacting hard over a small surface area.

THE TONFA

Having seen two of the less obvious ways in which the tonfas are used, we can now look at applications of some of the moves contained in the kata we have just practised.

Fig. 47 Here the high parry deflects the opponent's face punch. Notice how the right tonfa is held ready and 'cocked' against the ribs.

Fig. 48 The butt end of the right tonfa is thrust into the opponent's ribs.

THE TONFA

Fig. 49 The block takes the opponent's punch clear of the face.

Fig. 50 Here the tonfa is swung down in a knee strike, the peg swivelling in your grip. This is often used as a diversionary strike, to create a window for a following and more deadly strike.

THE TONFA

Fig. 51 Here the tonfa is being used to reinforce the elbow in an upward travelling strike to the opponent's jaw.

Fig. 52 The tonfa is swung with a backhand movement into the side of the opponent's head.

THE TONFA

Fig. 53 Use the tonfa to aggressively parry kicks. Here connection is made to the side of the kicking shin and not directly down on it.

Fig. 54 This type of upward swing isn't particularly powerful in terms of the impact generated but bearing in mind its target, it doesn't need to be!

THE TONFA

Fig. 55 *Right* The opponent's lower body is conveniently close for a butt end thrusting strike.

Fig. 56 *Below* Bar the opponent's thigh with your left tonfa and hook his Achilles tendon with the right.

Fig. 57 Striking with the peg end of the tonfa is particularly effective because it concentrates a great deal of force over a small area.

THE TONFA

Fig. 58 Here the left baton is being used to ram the opponent's head back. If you practise this with a partner, be very careful not to strike his throat!

Fig. 59 This shows clearly how the opponent is controlled by a throat bar as you hook his leading foot. He cannot withdraw his head because the right baton is holding him securely.

THE TONFA

Fig. 60 The opponent, still under control, is brought to the mat.

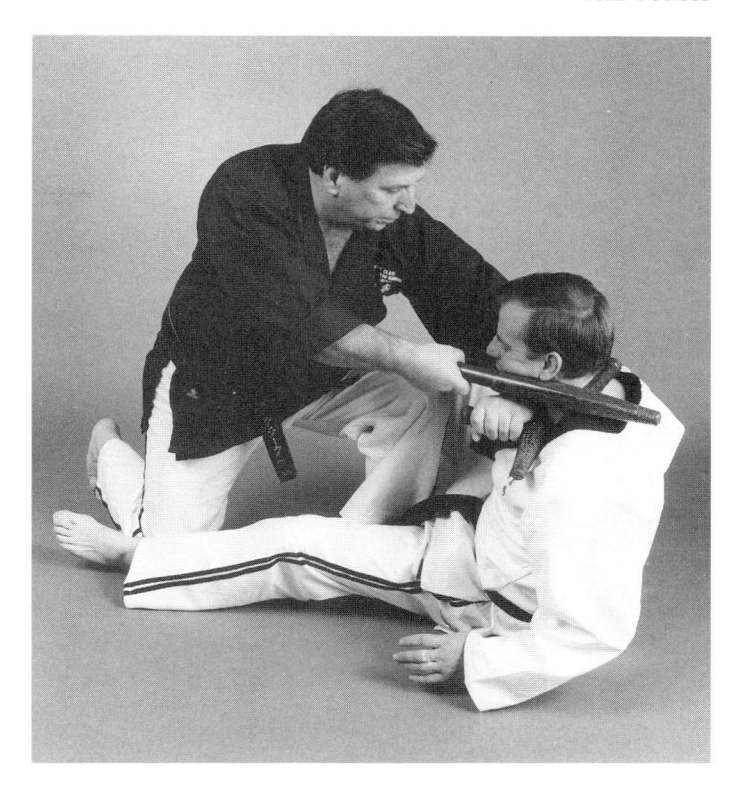

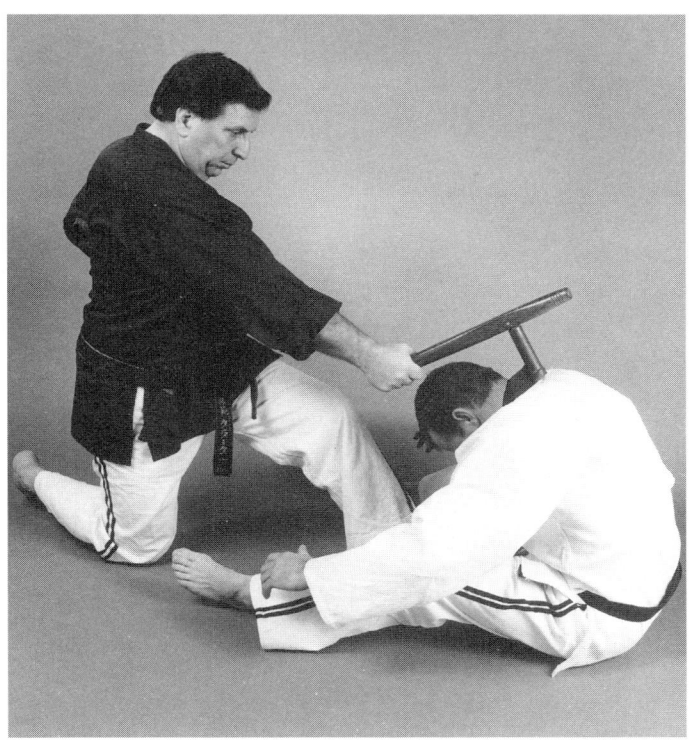

Fig. 61 Again the peg is used in a strike, this time against the base of the neck.

45

THE TONFA

Fig. 62 The opponent's body hook is blocked with a backhand movement of the right tonfa.

Fig. 63 The opponent's second punch is deflected upward by the slanted tonfa.

THE TONFA

Fig. 64 In a crisp action, the baton is swung down and back to defeat the final punch.

Fig. 65 Here both tonfas are used together in a double incurving strike to either side of the opponent's neck.

THE TONFA

Fig. 66 This time both pegs are used to strike the opponent's temples. Take care – this is a dangerous technique!

Fig. 67 The double thrusting butt-end strike seen here simultaneously attacks the base of the opponent's throat and the lower mid-section.

The above kata applications show quite clearly how versatile the tonfa is. When you have practised them a number of times with your partner, repeat the kata and this time see whether you can 'see' your partner in your mind's eye as you perform it.

Tonfa impact training drills

To practise these you will need a number of items, the first being a one-metre length of plastic cold-water pipe or broom handle. Both are light enough not to cause injury if they get past the tonfas, yet are hard enough to give the tonfa something to hit against. Your partner uses them as a baton, beginning with a downward strike on to your head (*see* fig. 45). At first the strike is made slowly, though it must always be on target so you learn how to cope with a strike coming directly at you. Once you can stop the strikes, then your partner can increase the force of his/her blows.

Then you have your partner thrust the butt end of the baton towards your mid-section. Step to the side and simultaneously turn your hips towards the thrust (after the manner of fig. 49). Use this action, coupled with a vertical tonfa, to deflect the baton to the side. When you can handle this, your partner thrusts the butt end into your face. Use the same type of block to deal with this, and also with circular swings that curve in towards your ribs and head. Finally, deflect attacks to the lower part of your body with a lower parry (*see* fig. 64).

In each case, the fact you are applying the tonfa to a baton means you can use considerable power in the deflection.

The second range of training drills requires a suspended bag, or a partner holding a large kicking pad or air-shield. Kicking pads are large, flat oblongs of plastazote closed cell foam (same as that used in swimming flotation pads). Several layers of these are heat-sealed together, sometimes with a layer of softer, more absorbent foam in the middle. The whole is enclosed within a tough vinyl covering. Your partner holds the pad firmly while you practise a series of full power strikes against it, paying particular attention to swivel strikes such as those practised in figs 50 and 54.

The nunchaku

Introduction

The nunchaku takes up a great deal of space when it is being whirled about, so make sure your practice area isn't crowded and check there are no low light fittings. As with the tonfa, the best way to learn the various techniques and applications is through a kata, the most basic of which is shown on the following pages. Keeping control over the moving baton is the most difficult part of nunchaku practice and it is also one of the most important. A strike which misses the target must be quickly retrieved so that a follow-up can be launched. This involves catching the moving baton, which in turn necessitates having your hand in the right place at the right time. The least painful way of learning how to do this is using the lightweight safety-chuk, though this has different ballistics to the flail.

The nunchaku kata

Fig. 68 Stand to attention, with head held high. Hold both batons of the nunchaku in your right hand. Let both arms hang naturally.

Fig. 69 *Above* Step back with your right foot and bring your left arm up and forward in a fend-off. Turn the palm forward-facing.

Fig. 70 *Above, right* Bring both batons around to the front, taking one in each hand. Pull the batons apart so the linkage becomes taut. Though this looks rather fancy, you will see later that it has a real practical value.

Fig. 71 *Right* Loop the left baton around your right elbow, so the right hand is close to the side of your head and the left is near your right armpit.

THE NUNCHAKU

Fig. 72 Release your left hand and swing the baton down. At this point, some people insert an additional strike as a way of improving dexterity. If you choose to do this, then don't stop at the lowest point; simply whip the baton around and down again for a double strike. All vertical strikes can be doubled in this way, and doubles should only be attempted once you can manage the single swing/catch.

Fig. 73 Even as the free baton reaches the lowest point of the strike, it is quickly retrieved for a single or double upward strike.

THE NUNCHAKU

Fig. 74 Bring the baton back so it loops over your right shoulder once more and is caught near the armpit with your left hand.

Fig. 75 Bring the flail around and across in front of your face and pull the batons apart in a blocking/trapping move.

THE NUNCHAKU

The second sequence is a mirror image of the first.

Fig. 76 *Left* Quickly move the link over your left triceps, so the left baton is high. Keep hold of the lower baton with your right hand.

Fig. 77 *Below, left* Strike vertically downward by releasing your right grip. Don't stop at the lowest point of the swing; simply whip the baton around and down again for an optional double strike.

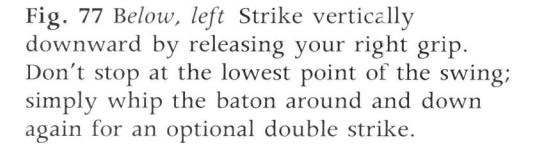

Fig. 78 *Below* Bring the baton up and perhaps around a second time before catching the free baton in your left armpit with the waiting hand.

THE NUNCHAKU

Fig. 79 *Above* Open the batons in front of you, stretching the link to trap a descending strike.

Fig. 80 *Above, right* Hook the flexible link over the back of someone's neck.

Fig. 81 *Right* Pull the opponent's head forward with the link and perform a right front kick to their mid-section.

THE NUNCHAKU

Fig. 82 *Above* A hard kick in the stomach would be expected to double the opponent forward, so pull them to your right and down to the mat.

Fig. 83 *Above, right* Turn your hips clockwise and lean away, looping the batons over your right shoulder.

Fig. 84 *Right* Wind your hips forward and release your left grip, so the flail whips around the front of the body.

Fig. 85 Allow a full follow-through, so the free baton loops around your back.

Fig. 86 In one seamless movement, unwind the other way and make a back hand cut with the baton.

THE NUNCHAKU

Fig. 87 The baton swings around and behind your body and is caught with your left hand which is waiting for it in the small of your back.

Fig. 88 Transfer your weight back on to your right foot.

THE NUNCHAKU

Fig. 89 Slide out with your left foot and jab with the butt of the left baton.

Fig. 90 Release the right baton.

THE NUNCHAKU

Fig. 91 *Above* Strike upward with a single or double circular movement, catching with the right hand under the left shoulder blade.

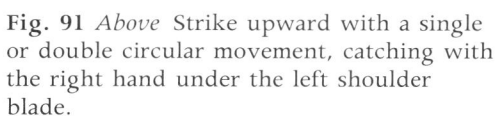

Fig. 92 *Above, right* Release the left baton.

Fig. 93 *Right* Strike with a single/double circular movement, catching with the left hand under the right armpit.

THE NUNCHAKU

Fig. 94 *Right* Strike down with the right baton.

Fig. 95 *Below* Bring the baton back up and catch it with your left hand.

Fig. 96 *Below, right* Hold the rice flail steady as you pivot clockwise to face the front, left foot leading.

Fig. 97 *Above* Release your right hand and strike upward with the left baton.

Fig. 98 *Above, right* Catch with your right hand near your left armpit.

Fig. 99 *Right* Release the left baton and strike upward in a single or double circle.

Fig. 100 Catch with your left hand close to the right armpit.

Fig. 101 Release your right hand and strike diagonally downward and across your body.

THE NUNCHAKU

Fig. 102 *Above* Catch the free right baton behind your back.

Fig. 103 *Above, right* Step up and bring your feet together.

Fig. 104 *Right* Bring the two batons together and take them both in your right hand.

Applications of the techniques used in the kata

Fig. 105 The rice flail is generally used in a mid- to long-range mode (though it can be used from shorter distances) and this being the case, one of the things you must do is create distance. In this case, step back and thrust your left palm toward the opponent.

Fig. 106 Though each baton is relatively short, the ballistics produced through the flexible linkage are quite awesome! The loose baton whips through the air and can cause serious injury. This is why it makes good sense to practise with safety-chuks until you have acquired some skill.

THE NUNCHAKU

Fig. 107 *Above* Practise so you can develop power on the upstroke too but don't lose control of the free baton!

Fig. 108 *Above, right* The flexible linkage between batons is ideal for trapping the opponent's limbs or weapons. Stretch the batons apart and allow the impact to close them.

Fig. 109 *Right* Loop the flexible linkage over the back of the opponent's head, taking his arm back too.

THE NUNCHAKU

Fig. 110 The last thing you want to do is stand on one leg so close to the opponent, so snap kick him in the groin or mid-section, making your kick as quickly as you can.

Fig. 111 *Below* The kick collapses the opponent forward, making it relatively easy to bring him down to the mat.

THE NUNCHAKU

Fig. 112 The full power backhand strike is particularly forceful and therefore more difficult to retrieve afterward.

Fig. 113 You have collected the free baton with your left hand, only to have an opponent seize your left wrist.

Fig. 114 Use your body weight to lunge forward, driving the butt end of the left baton into the opponent's solar plexus. The opponent will have been pulling on your wrist, so this attack is unopposed.

Fig. 115 Now shift your weight back to open distance and swing the rice flail in an upward strike.

Practise these various applications with a partner and then have another go at the kata. This time imagine your partner in your mind's eye as you perform the techniques. It is important that you understand all the applications since they give the kata a real purpose and meaning.

THE NUNCHAKU

Nunchaku impact training drills

Practise controlling your strikes by aiming against a partner. As you might imagine, this requires a fair amount of skill so it is probably better if you begin by using safety-chuks. Use only a low amount of muscle power and aim to pull the baton just short of a strike. But do bear in mind that suddenly reversing the action causes the free baton to whiplash, so allow for this with your aim-point. Increase delivery speed gradually and **only once you are 100% accurate**. Then switch to normal rice flails but allow for their greater weight and consequently different ballistics. Again, begin slowly and gradually build up the force of your delivery, **but only once you are 100% accurate**.

Fig. 116 Begin with a backhand strike. Your partner stands with hands clasped behind his head. Take the flail across your body and note the left hand which extends forward in a guarding position.

THE NUNCHAKU

Fig. 117 Begin with a low strike which curls around the back of your partner's calves.

Fig. 118 Retrieve the baton and bring it back across your front. Then curl a second strike around your partner's back.

THE NUNCHAKU

Fig. 119 Retrieve the baton and make your third strike to the back of your partner's head. Now work in reverse order, striking next to the back, then to the back of the legs.

The object in this exercise is to move slowly, unrolling the baton and then curling it back again in a smooth action. Accurate targeting is essential!

Fig. 120 Use the same drill to practise your forehand horizontal strike but always remember to aim at targets on the back of your opponent's body, not on his front!

The free baton behaves differently when it hits a target than when it is simply swung through the air. Get in some impact practice by swinging the baton into an air-shield, a kicking bag, a suspended bag or even a strong wooden staff.

Fig. 121 Practise upward strike against a horizontal staff.

Fig. 122 Your partner must make sure that the staff is held well away from his head and body. Here a downward strike is being used.

THE NUNCHAKU

Fig. 123 Hold the staff vertically and practise horizontal swings against it.

Fig. 124 Make sure you don't catch your partner's fingers!

The police tonfa

Introduction

The police tonfa, or 'side-handled baton' as it is generally called, is now a standard item of equipment in Britain's police forces. It came to Britain from the USA where it has enjoyed a certain degree of success. The police tonfa is not easy to use and the training schemes implemented by the Home Office leave something to be desired.

In this section some of the more advanced applications of the single tonfa are shown, using a baton supplied by the Royal Canadian Police. These are all effective restraint techniques and all require a considerable degree of dexterity before they can be used in combat situations. Please note: the applications involving throat bars are potentially dangerous!

Applications

Fig. 125 The opponent takes up a knife in the right hand. Step back with your right foot to draw you back out of range. Now the opponent must step to reach you, and the step will serve as a warning. Hold the long baton near its end, with the peg turned inward-facing.

Fig. 126 The opponent slides forward on his left foot and stabs downward. The slide forward is a cue. Go to meet the opponent and deflect the knife strike early on.

THE POLICE TONFA

Fig. 127 Slide the tonfa under your opponent's right arm and over his shoulder. Hook the peg around his forearm. Take the peg and bar his arm back. Increase leverage by drawing on the baton with your right arm.

Fig. 128 Apply enough leverage and the opponent will drop the knife.

THE POLICE TONFA

Fig. 129 Deflect the opponent's body hook with your left forearm. Again, it is important to correctly set up the distance between you as the first step of any response. Draw the tonfa back.

Fig. 130 Reach over the top of the opponent's right arm and snag his elbow with the peg.

THE POLICE TONFA

Fig. 131 Pull the tonfa across so you flex the opponent's elbow, barring his wrist with yours. Use a combination of tonfa action and wrist pressure to fold his right arm up his back.

Fig. 132 Keeping your left arm in contact with his, step around behind the opponent and catch his throat with the peg. Draw him upright by pulling on the peg.

THE POLICE TONFA

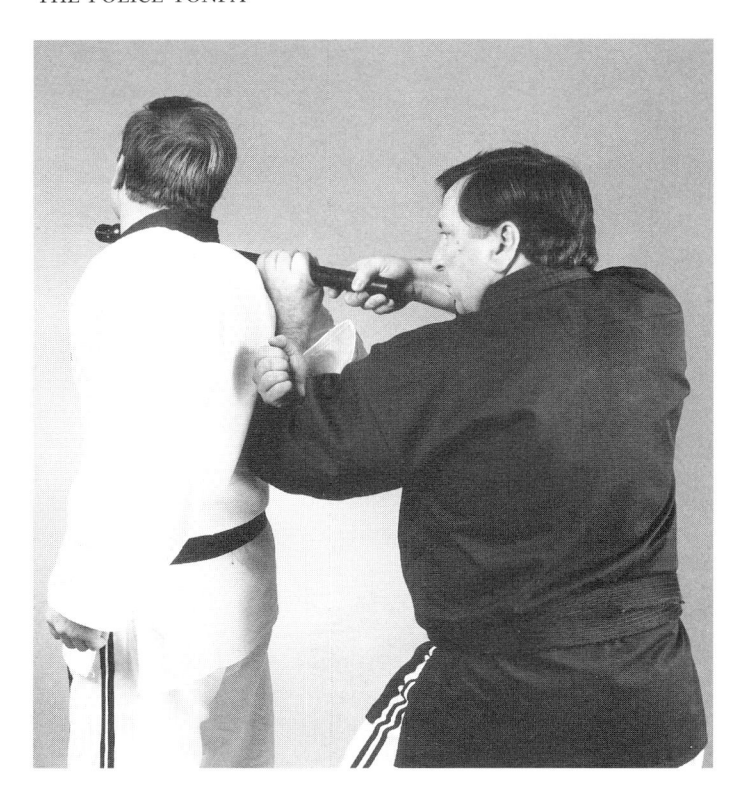

Fig. 133 This shows the position of your arms from the other side as you apply the throat bar.

Fig. 134 Stop the opponent's hook with a cross block. A powerful block can be very punishing when reinforced with a tonfa baton!

THE POLICE TONFA

Fig. 135 Twist your hips toward the opponent and loop the baton around the back of his neck, using the peg as a swivel.

Fig. 136 Reach across with your left hand and take hold of the baton. Apply a scarf hold but be careful! This closes off the carotid arteries supplying the brain, leading to rapid unconsciousness. So watch your partner carefully.

THE POLICE TONFA

Fig. 137 Block the opponent's punch with your lead hand.

Fig. 138 Keep your left hand in the fend-off position while you snag the opponent's neck with the peg.

THE POLICE TONFA

Fig. 139 Slide your left forearm forward so it jams across the opponent's throat. Hold the baton firmly to prevent it sliding loose.

Fig. 140 Use body evasion and a downward left parry to deflect the opponent's front kick. Do not meet the opponent's fast rising shin square-on with your forearm, because the chances are his shin will win!

THE POLICE TONFA

Fig. 141 Keep your left wrist in contact with the opponent's shin and hook the back of his knee. Don't bring your face too near to his fists!

Fig. 142 Turn the opponent round, hooking your left forearm under his shin. Take hold of the free end of the baton.

THE POLICE TONFA

Fig. 143 *Right* This next step is quite complicated. First take the opponent to the mat. Then step over the baton with your left foot and sink down on to your right knee. Keep hold of the tonfa in your right hand and the other end jams against your left Achilles tendon. Take the opponent's toes in your left hand and push them forward. Stop when he slaps the mat!

Fig. 144 *Left* You can also use the tonfa to apply pressure to nerve points. This achieves effective results without the need for cracking the opponent over the head!

The above techniques were taken at random from a selection of more advanced techniques which will form the basis of a future book. They clearly show the versatility of the tonfa as an effective weapon in today's society.

The nunchaku – advanced applications

In the final section of this book, we are going to look at some fairly advanced techniques using the rice flail.

Fig. 145 Begin by stopping the opponent's punch with your lead hand. Carry the flails in your right hand.

THE NUNCHAKU – ADVANCED APPLICATIONS

Fig. 146 Loop the flails over your opponent's head but move quickly because he isn't going to stand still for you!

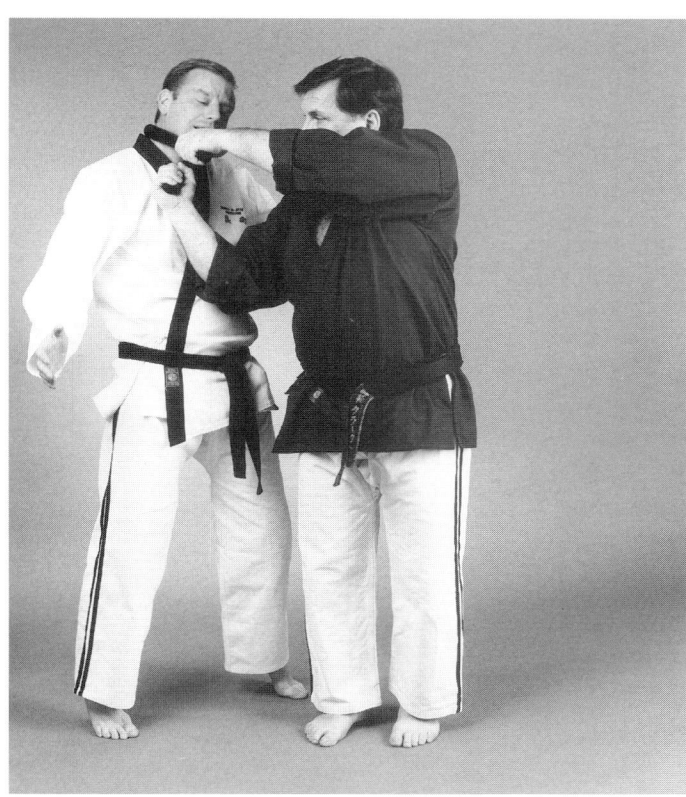

Fig. 147 Step up and around, closing the batons either side of the opponent's throat. This compresses the carotid arteries, so be careful!

THE NUNCHAKU – ADVANCED APPLICATIONS

Fig. 148 Drop on to your left knee but maintain the scarf hold. Slide your right foot out to bar the opponent's shins and draw him forward.

Fig. 149 Step to the side and use both batons together to deflect the opponent's punch.

THE NUNCHAKU – ADVANCED APPLICATIONS

Fig. 150 Quickly whip the linkage over his head and apply pressure to the carotids.

Fig. 151 Stamp down behind the opponent's knee to drop him. Maintain your grip on the batons.

THE NUNCHAKU – ADVANCED APPLICATIONS

Fig. 152 Step back and pull the opponent on to his back.

Fig. 153 Pull the batons free and make ready to strike downward into the opponent's groin.

THE NUNCHAKU – ADVANCED APPLICATIONS

Fig. 154 The opponent throws a hook at your body. Block it with the flexible linkage.

Fig. 155 Trap the opponent's wrist by closing the batons on it, and rotate your lead foot outward.

THE NUNCHAKU – ADVANCED APPLICATIONS

Fig. 156 Step through with your right foot and block the opponent's right-handed punch with your right wrist.

Fig. 157 This photograph is taken from a slightly different angle. Step around and behind the opponent with your left foot and drop on to your left knee. Extend your right leg and draw the opponent backward and over it. Be careful not to cut or friction burn your partner's throat with this technique!

THE NUNCHAKU – ADVANCED APPLICATIONS

Fig. 158 Lastly, trap the opponent's front kick with the flexible linkage. Hold the batons firmly or they will be jarred loose from your grasp.

Fig. 159 Close the batons on his foot and turn him round.

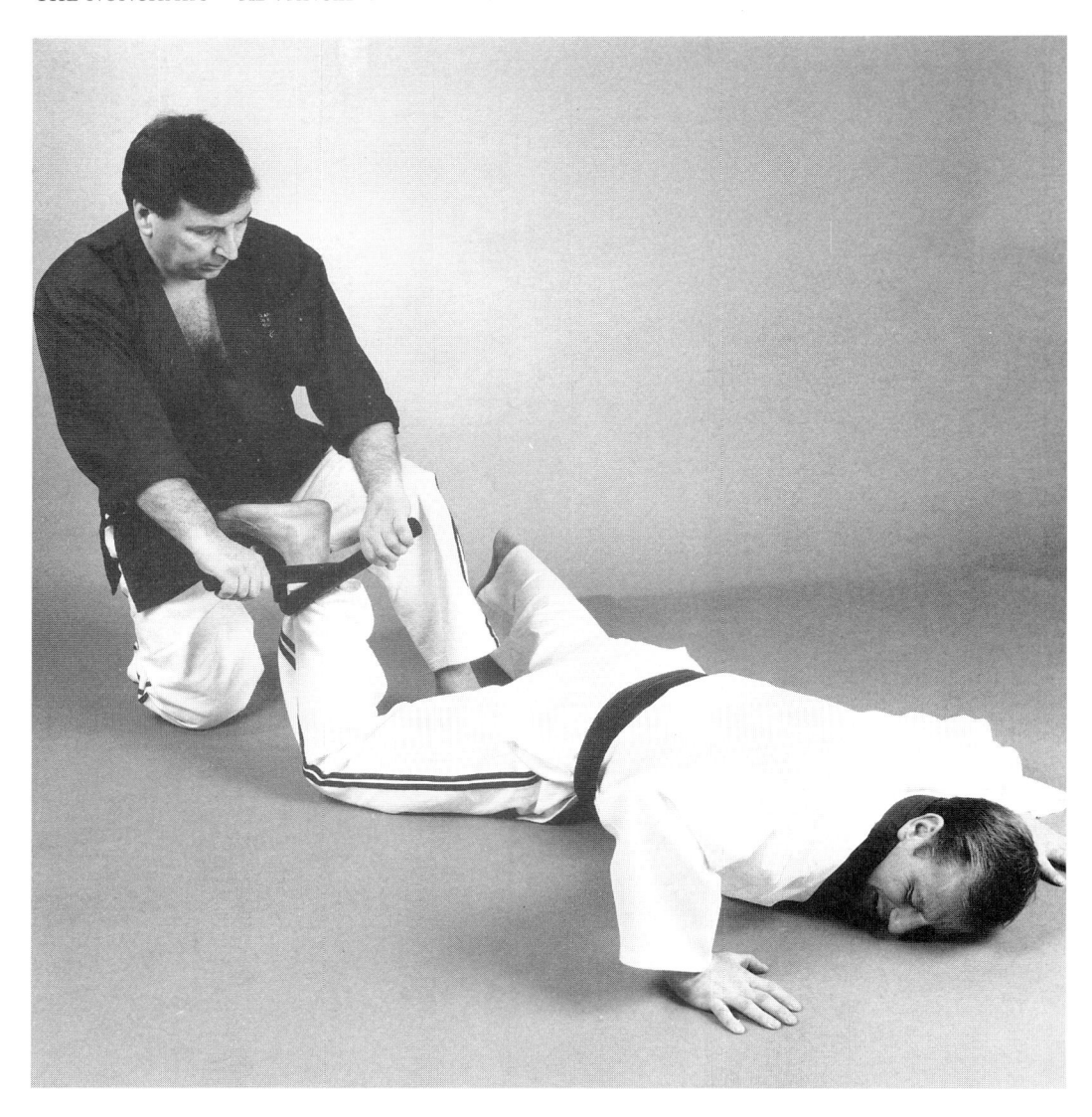

Fig. 160 Closing the batons causes severe pain and ensures the opponent's compliance as you take him down to the mat and on to his face.

THE NUNCHAKU – ADVANCED APPLICATIONS

Fig. 161 Finish by swapping your left hand for your left foot! Tread on the baton to maintain closure and apply pressure to the opponent's foot with your left hand. Stop the instant he taps up!

And finally...

I hope you have enjoyed using this publication and that it will help you remember the moves of your weapon kata. But remember: you can't learn everything from a book because it can't tell you if you are doing something wrong. So train regularly in your WKO club and use the manual to help you remember what has been taught.

I'm sure you'll also be interested in the companion book which is currently being planned. This will show you how to use the *sai* (fig. 162) and the six-foot *staff* (fig. 163).

Good training!

Robert Clark

Fig. 162

Fig. 163